INTRODUCTION

Welcome to this my seventh book in the AROUND series, which has been specially assembled ..... pictorially illustrate the hamlets, villages, and larger communities to the east of Bristol as they appeared in the past, either within living memory, or previously when those older pictures can give us a small, but significant insight to what life and the community was like a hundred years or more ago. Last year I produced and published a book entitled "Around Warmley", which brought the reader close if not just over the boundary of Kingswood, and thus this book continues the visual story into the heart of the parish and onto and through the Bristol boundary.

The Kings Wood is of course a very ancient area that covered a very much larger part of southern Gloucestershire than the area that is today recognized as the district of Kingswood, and its history is synonymous with it being the playground of the royal families of England. Kept for the sole preserve of royal hunting parties, whose main aim in life was to enjoy themselves as much as possible, whilst playing havoc with the local wild life, both human and animal. In the course of time, the ruthless hunting antics of the royals began to wane, more and more trees were cut down to help build a Navy, and gradually the reduced forest became a haven for entrepreneurs, aided and abetted by those who chose or were forced to live outside of the law. Odd pockets of coal had always been found on or just under the surface of the ground, but little attention had been paid to it, when the forest itself provided all the fuel needed. However with the progress of mankind came the ever increasing need to find improved sources of fuel, and this is where the entrepreneurs stepped in, to exploit for their financial benefit the extraction of this "black gold", and who better to do the hard dangerous work of digging out this fuel than those who were using the sanctity of the forest to escape the clutches of the law. Gradually the remains of the forest were destroyed, the coal, and other minerals extracted, and new industries appeared, whilst over the same period of time, the inhabitants became less lawless, the miners became more religious, small isolated pockets of communities expanded and merged with each other, and then in turn absorbed the overspill of people from nearby Bristol. Kingswood became synonymous with shoes, motor cycles and light engineering, but nowadays there is no one particular industry for which Kingswood can be proud, instead whilst it does employ many people within its boundaries, it has predominantly become a dormitory area of vast housing estates, whilst struggling to keep its independence.

As always, my very special thanks go to Doreen my wife for her help and encouragement during a rather traumatic period in her life. I would also like to acknowledge the help and materials provided by Mike Tozer, and Janet & Derek Fisher as without their co-operation many of the pictures included would not have been seen. At all times I have endeavoured to minimize any mistakes made, but should any exist then they are of my own making for which I apologise, and trust that they will not distract your pleasure in reading this book.

March 2004   Ian S Bishop

When my book *AROUND WARMLEY* was prepared, an incorrect picture and caption appeared on page 36, when instead of showing this illustration the Charlton Road Garage was shown by mistake. To help correct the error this book starts in Warmley with a most interesting c1930 composition of the actual ROP garage in Deanery Road. Petrol in those days could be sold through an extension arm, which went over the pavement, and obviously no one considered there to be any extra danger from the adjoining gas lit street lamp, or the on the premise smoking. The car on the left is AHW316, whilst the pick-up truck is registered HW4095.

Cadbury Heath School on the junction with Wraxall Road and Cadbury Heath Road, on the 27th July 1990, not long before it was demolished and replaced with a new style school. The entrance nearest the camera was originally designated solely for girls and infants, so that they could be kept separate from the nasty rough boys when they went to and from school.

Although the quality of the picture is not that good, this is a very rare and interesting picture of the rank of two storied cottages built in Tower Lane to house Champion's employees during the nineteenth century. Taken around 1930, these buildings were demolished and all that remains of their existence is a fenced car park.

Prior to the breakthrough when Tower Lane was still a cul-de-sac, and Dalton Young was still in production, although their demise is not that far away. Houses have already begun to appear on the other side of the divide where once there were open fields, and in a year or so both sections of Tower Lane will be connected to form an important and busy link to the Ring Road. As far as the building on the right is concerned it will, after much time and effort, form the nucleus of the Kingswood Museum. Picture dated 2nd March 1991

The new part of Tower Lane as it leads towards a roundabout and the connection with a short section of Wraxall Road and ultimately the Ring Road itself. The newly built houses overlook the recently landscaped bank that separates the buildings from the pavement. 2nd March 1991

Looking down Hill Street on a bright spring afternoon in the middle of April 1989, with as a backdrop the hills, which form the most southerly part of the Cotswolds as they head for the northern fringes of Bath. Although the number of vehicles on the road is increasing, they have still not yet reached the levels of the twenty-first century.

The large bay villas contrast with their less pretentious neighbours, as part of the variety of home architecture in Hill Street, which was developed at the start of the last century, especially those constructed at the top of the hill. In the background is a more modern stark brick concept of home living with little or no character, looking totally out of place. 11th March 1989.

The "Old Flowerpot Inn", relaxing in the heat of the summer in between opening hours.
28 August 1986.

Taken from just below the brow of the hill where High Street stops and Hill Street begins with the latter sweeping down towards Warmley and the countryside beyond. With the tramcar terminus behind the camera, and with only the occasional bus through to Wick, from here on the locals had to walk, with some taking the "short-cut" over the fields behind the right-hand properties if they were going to Cadbury Heath, or Oldland. c1920.

Car 135 stands at the Kingswood terminus, waiting to make the return journey to Old Market, whilst the storm clouds of an imminent war hang over like a ladened sky. The entrance to the tram depot is to the left of the car; on the right there is an advertisement, which tells us that Will Hay is appearing in the film *"Ask a Policemen"* at the Regent Cinema. 4th August 1939.

Taken on the same day, on the right is a view from the front of the open top deck of the tram, which has just arrived from Old Market, whilst it waits to move onto the single track currently occupied by car 135. From this angle it is possible to see the track, which leads into the depot as it swings away to the left from the tram just in front of the man with the bicycle.

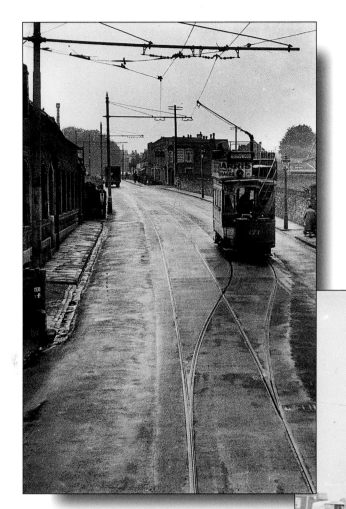

Looking back in the opposite direction this time from the tramcar waiting on the single track, as car 171 comes to the end of its journey up the long drag from Old Market, just after a summer shower has passed. All of the buildings shown in this illustration still remain, with others having now been constructed in the open spaces. Apart from the new buildings, it is only the density of the traffic, and the absence of the tram and its accoutrements that mark the main difference with today's view. 4th August 1939.

The picture below was taken a year earlier, when it was still possible for the tramcars from Kingswood to operate right through to the "Tramway Centre". A few passengers sit aboard car 126, whilst the single deck bus service through to Wick trundles into view. With an

absence of any buildings on the right of the picture a semi rural feel to the scene would be achieved, accept for the existence of the gas street lighting August 1938

The low winter sunshine of 1940 picks out the tramcars housed in the Kingswood Depot, all now with white painted bumper bars, and hooded lights as part of the need to operate after dark through the black-out conditions then in force.

With the rush to rid Bristol of its trams, most of the system was declared redundant during the latter part of the 1930's and in order that the vehicles could be easily broken-up, it was decided to cut a hole in the rear of Kingswood Depot and lay temporary track in the field, so that the surplus trams could be taken through. This can be clearly seen in the picture on the right, with car 57 waiting its turn. August 1939.

A trilogy of pictures recording the demise of what was, during the first three decades of the last century, a fine commuter service that radiated out into the suburbs of Bristol, a city which once could claim that the largest fleet of open top tramcars in the Country operated through its streets. In the top picture, taken in early August 1939, at least eighteen trams are lined up to await their fate, with all of them likely to be broken up by the end of the following month. Top right shows car 57, whilst below is a rare view of a works car, as normally this vehicle would only venture out into the public domain at night as it was responsible for grinding any rough edges off the tram line, and to keep them as smooth as possible. These pictures were also taken during the first week of August 1939, and within a month of the start of the Second World War.

The old crossroads in the centre of Syston Common, in the days not so long ago when it was possible to drive across the common both north and south and east and west. The construction of the Ring Road stopped all that, with the removal of the old road bridge over the railway, and now this area is much more isolated. On the right is the cottage, which stood on the cross roads for many years, just prior to its demolition. 18th April 1989.

A gathering of Wesleyans arrange themselves at the junction of Anchor Road and Fisher Road, (New Cheltenham) to have their picture taken before they move off under the Made for Ever, Wesley Chapel Sunday School banner together with their decorated float to join the annual Whitsuntide Procession sometime during the early 1920's. The idea of having a chapel in Anchor Road was first considered during the early part of the 1890's, when the house at 44 Syston Common was found to be too small for the number of people wishing to attend the Bible class. After purchasing the necessary land, the foundation stone was laid on the 15th July 1896, and after experiencing a number of financial problems in meeting the cost of £276.50, the chapel was opened in March 1897, with the first sermon taken by Daniel Flook on the 11th April 1897.

Yew Tree Farm, Chiphouse Lane, Lower Soundwell circa 1897, just after the chickens had been fed.

Having seen the various ways of reaching Kingswood from the eastern villages it overlooks, we are now back in the High Street, near the junction with Alma Road. With the Kingswood School, built in1892 to accommodate 210 pupils dominating the left-hand side of the picture, and the church tower in the background, the only vehicles are horse-drawn, of which two of them seem to be well and truly ladened. Note the fine tracery of the post bracket holding up the electric wires. c1903.

HIGH ST. KINGSWOOD.

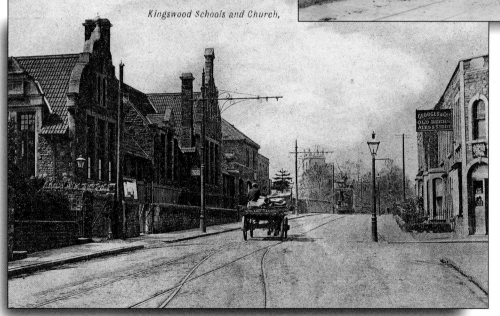

Kingswood Schools and Church,

On the left the camera has been moved closer to John Hayes' Off Sales shop, which sells George's Beers, on the corner of Alma Road, adjacent to where the tram track changes from single line working, to double track so as to facilitate trams being able to pass each other at the terminus a few hundred yards down the road. With the Midland Railway carter and his charge trying to imitate being a tram, the real thing heads towards the church, and the start of the downward journey to the centre of Bristol. Note the nearest gas lamp has been positioned away from the curb, and is in fact standing in the roadway. c1910.

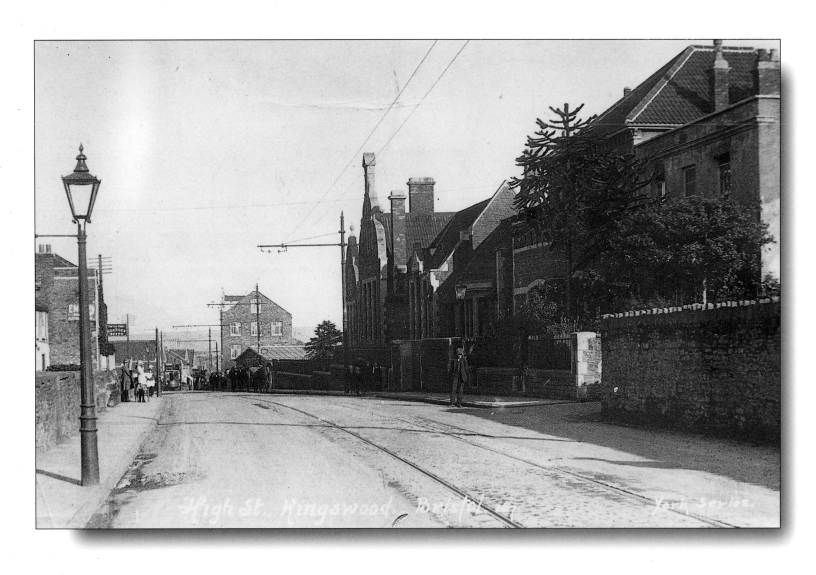

High St., Kingswood, Bristol

Having come over the brow of a slight climb from the tram terminus, we can now look back the way we have come, passed the Kingswood School ~ later known as Park Primary School ~ on the right. The High Street is still lit by gas, but with large gaps in between each lamp, the street must have been full of dark shadows after sunset. c1910

18

Kingswood High Street in the reverse direction, on a rather dull summer's day when most people appeared to have decided to walk away from the centre of the newly developing town. With just one loan cyclist heading in the opposite direction, alongside the stonewall, which hides the ground that will be laid out as a park, this main road is devoid of traffic, a scene that would be very difficult to replicate today. c1925

High St. Kingswood.

HIGH ST KINGSWOOD .636

The season has changed, as has the angle and the position of the camera. Here we can see that the road behind the photographer has widened sufficiently to allow the tram tracks, set in their cobbled road to double allowing tramcars to pass each other as they ply their trade to and from Bristol. Holy Trinity Church stands out through the leafless trees, as the winter sun casts feeble shadows across the highway, occupied by one loan carter, with the word HOWELIGHT on the tailboard. c1912.

Three individual pictures of Kingswood Park, which help to demonstrate the civic pride the local council must have felt in creating such a peaceful setting in an oasis of exquisite horticulture. Top left is probably a 1950's view looking past the newly replaced gates that open out onto the High Street. Below, the photographer has, around 1939, caught the attention of nearly all of the visitors to the park as they idle away the day sitting in the

THE PARK, KINGSWOOD

2

KINGSWOOD PARK.

spring sunshine contemplating the threat of war clouds hanging overhead. With the probability that the war will include air raids, the machine to sound the warning and all clear can be seen on top of the tallest building in the background. The picture on the right was postally used after that conflict, but is probably based upon a pre-war photograph.

20

Kingswood citizens relax in the bright spring sunshine amongst the civic pride of a well-tended amenity, with tidy paths, neatly trimmed lawns, all free of rubbish, graffiti and vandalism, even dogs are not permitted to run loose, as they must be under control at all times. No doubt the subject of conversation on most of their lips was the gathering of the storm clouds that herald the start of the Second World War, how so much was to change! c1939

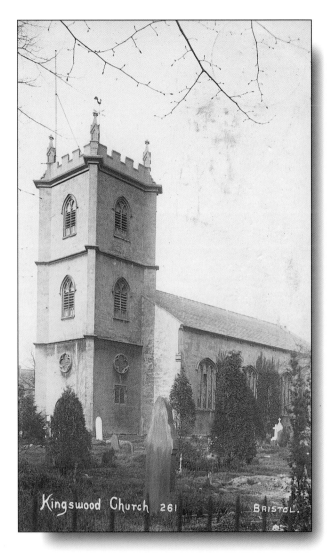

Three different views of Holy Trinity Church, with top left a broadside picture of the northern side taken from across the road in High Street with the main gates in the centre, whilst below is the picturesque aspect of the attractive interior, On the right is a view of the southerly side of the church, looking across the churchyard towards the main road. All c 1910

Looking up Church Road to the junction with High Street, and across to the tower of Holy Trinity. Note the dominance of the double yellow lines.

Opposite a self explanatory card giving publicity to the Old Tabernacle

Old Tabernacle, Kingswood.

Built by George Whitefield, with the assistance of John Cennick (the hymn writer) A.D. 1741.

This was the first of a number of Churches erected by Whitefield, who is said to have been "the greatest religious orator since apostolic days."

It was in this immediate neighbourhood, February, 1739, that he broke away from the conventional religion of his time and commenced his great open-air revival.

HIGH STREET, KINGSWOOD

With the camera taking us further into Kingswood, tramcar 182 has just reached the point where for the first time since leaving the city centre, the route is downhill. On this bright autumn day, with Church Road off on the right, and the churchyard wall on the left, the shaded newsagent has a board outside his shop that reads *"Astounding Evidence at TITANIC enquiry"*. c1912.

"HIGH STREET, KINGSWOOD."

On that same bright autumn day, as seen in the picture on page 24, the camera has been moved a hundred yards or so along the road in the way in which it was originally facing, and then reversed so that we are now able to look back to where we have been. By now the photographer has attracted a large crowd of young lads, most of who have decided to stand in the road at the junction with Church Road, whilst others strike individual pose in front of shops that will at sometime in the future become the Linden Hotel. c1912.

HIGH ST KINGSWOOD. 634.

The strong summer sunshine casts deep shadows across the roadway just at the place where the tramlines take on the dual capacity of allowing tramcars to pass each other in safety. The sunblinds have been pulled out to shade many of the shop windows on the right, although in the middle of the picture one blind has become detached from its box and now lies spread-eagled across the pavement. Apart from that all looks peaceful and harmonious in Kingswood at this time. c1912

The young man, who may or may not be a friend of the photographer, was determined to ensure that his picture was taken, although he probably did not realise that his posture would be frozen in time and that it would be seen by subsequent generations yet to come. The *Queen's Head* is to the left, whilst G. & H.T. Cowles advertise their Saddle and Harness making business. On the right a pony and trap ambles along, having a few moments ago calmly dealt with a passing tram. Whilst one or two others are also interested in the antics of the cameraman, the majority of the locals are simply getting on with their own business. c1905

High St, Kingswood, Bristol. 359.

The antics of the photographer have attracted the curiosity of a group of small children, without realising that this particular moment in their lives was about to be captured forever. As for the adults they are not quite so sure that the cameraman should be there, and in any case they really have no great desire to be in the photograph. With Hanham Road off to the left and Regent Street straight ahead, we are almost at the centre of Kingswood as it bathes in the contentment of the warm summer sunshine. C1908

Having crossed the street, the camera has been turned around to show the view looking back the way we have come. A lone cyclist negotiates his journey so as to avoid ending up cycling along the tramlines, passing as he does a small group of people outside the Post Office and the Bristol Co-operative Society shop, both just visible on the extreme right of the previous picture. Diadem Flour, which is locally produced in nearby Bristol, is prominently advertised. c1907

Looking across the lawn to the rather gaunt lines of the Community Centre that contrasts in mood and in architecture with the perpendicular shapes incorporated in the adjoining building. c1936

Unfortunately there are no explanations behind either of these two pictures but the well-known local photographer, Mr W G Plucknett, who traded from 36 Regent Street, took both in and around the Kingswood Community Centre. c1935

If any reader can identify the events, and put names to any of the participants, please contact the author. On the back of the card from which the right-hand picture has been taken it states Hilda and Ethel English, of Zion Place, Syston Park, if that is any clue.

Tennis Courts, The Park, Kingswood

"Anyone for Tennis"? Could be the caption for this particular picture, although most of the spectators seem more interested in what is going on across the road, as the photographer faces his camera looking down The Park, and freezes a moment in time for posterity. c1920

The splendid villas occupy this rather select corner of "The Park", Kingswood, which together with Southfield Avenue almost formed a complete circle with parkland views subsequently occupied by the construction of Southey Avenue, and beyond the development of the post-war New Cheltenham housing estate. c1923.

The Park, Kingswood
Bristol. 372

An aerial view taken from the top of the church tower around 1904, with the Wesleyan Church dominating its surroundings.

Although the exact reason behind the erection of this floral "gateway" at the point where High Street becomes Regent Street and where they form a junction with Hanham Road and Park Road, is not known, it is believed to be part of the celebrations to commemorate Queen Victoria's Diamond Jubilee in 1897.

This fine edifice built on the corner of Regent street and Hanham Road must have seemed, when it was first constructed to house both Lloyds Bank and a hotel, to have been a truly magnificent building totally out of character with its surrounding, but at the time a new century had not long dawned, and Britain was still the mightiest country in the world, therefore why not build such a structure. Taken from a card postally used on the 7th January 1904

With the camera having been taken back a few feet, and slightly repositioned, we can now look down Regent Street across to the Lloyds Bank end of the building, and include the shop fronts on the opposite side of the street. On this occasion the photographer has just one interested spectator, as tramcar 178 breasts the climb up from the centre of Bristol, on the final section of its journey to the terminus. c1913.

PARR'S BANK AND THE CLOCK TOWER, KINGSWOOD.

It might be interesting to speculate that this picture was taken on the same day as the previous view, with the photographer having moved his position across and down the road so that he could turn his camera completely around and point towards Bristol, which is now the way that tramcar 178 is going. The summer sunshine has cast the left-hand Lloyds Bank building into deep shadow, in total contrast to the sunlit buildings on the right. Hanging in a prominent position is the sign of F. Moss Chemist   c1913

THE CLOCK TOWER. KINGSWOOD.

A7472.

As midday approaches, all seems peaceful and quiet as people go about their business, unhindered by either traffic or pollution. Hodders are now the chemists on the right, with Pearks grocery store on one side and Verrier the tailor on the other. There are no parking restrictions, and the road is wide enough for even the car on the right to park in safety away from passing trams. c1938

Hidden by the sunblind in the previous picture, here is a full frontal view of Pearks shop in Regent Street. Presumably the gentleman second in on the left, in a waistcoat, is the manager in this circa 1912 picture. Note the full window display and the various prices.

Perhaps one of Kingswood's most recognisable landmarks, The Clock Tower, erected in 1897 to celebrate Queen Victoria's sixty years on the throne of not only England, but the largest Empire ever known, an Empire on which the sun never set. At the time, Kingswood, like most of Great Britain was fairly prosperous, and confident of the future, in the safe and certain knowledge that her Navy ruled the waves, and very few would risk challenging Britain's supremacy. Little did they know that within twenty years, the whole world would be turned upside down with many of Kingswood's young men lost forever.

This c1954 view shows the Clock Tower in all its magnificence, flanked by the Clock Tower Fish Shop on the left, and the Golden Hart public house, on the right.

REGENT ST. KINGSWOOD. 632.

Although this picture has been taken from a card posted on the 5th August 1932, a close inspection of the clothes being worn almost certainly dates the actual picture having been constructed around 1903. Apart from a tram in the background, all of the other vehicles in the view are horse-drawn, hence the reason for the young lad in the left-hand shadow, armed with his bucket and shovel. Two Victorian style ladies glance across at the photographer with a certain stare of disapproval, whilst behind them and the horse and cart is the grocery shop of "Harris" with a large display of Lipton's Tea. Behind the lamppost is the entrance to London Street. Note the large Van Houten's advertisement for cocoa, as the citizens of Kingswood stroll along Regent Street in the midday sun.

Regent Street, Kingswood, Bristol. 1435.

Regent Street when the height of ladies fashion appears to be long white summer dresses, in which to stroll along the sunny side of the street to window shop and to be seen, although at present the photographer may have stolen their thunder as the nearby young men appear to be more interested in the actions of the photographer. Apart from numerous pedestrians, a pram, and two bicycles, there is a wonderful absence of traffic that would be hard to replicate today. c1908

Although the camera has gone back a few feet, the moment it has captured is many years ahead of the time shown in the previous picture. Much has happened during the intervening forty-years or so, including two World Wars, and a vastly changed society. The trams have gone, and more and more people are beginning to own their own car, but so far they are few and far between, and there is no need to impose restrictions upon their freedom of movement, as demonstrated by the parked Austin, and the early Morris Minor hogging the centre of the road. Nevertheless there are still many pedestrians out in the sunshine, who will catch the bus home. c1952

Jubilee Memorial. Kingswood.

The recently erected Jubilee Memorial Clock Tower dominates the right-hand section of this most interesting picture of Regent Street that at the time the photograph was taken still included, on the left, a rank of tired looking cottages two of which have had their front parlours turned into a small shop. A well dressed lady with a white fur collar and a "Gladstone" bag is about to step out of the left-hand shop doorway, whilst next-door Rossiter's appear to be closed. Further down the street, can be seen the sign for F Moss, Chemist. c1900

The old cottages depicted in the previous picture have now been replaced with a row of purpose built shops, which certainly appear to be better patronized. On the left is Henry Jas Flook's grocery shop, which has a well stocked window display highlighted by the bright sunshine. Next door, Alfred Haines has pulled out the blinds to prevent the fading of his stationery products. Just two cyclists and a handcart occupy what appears to be a rather dirty road surface. c1908

Regent St, Kingswood. Bristol. 266.   York Series.

Although the camera is in an almost identical position, to the previous photograph, there is much that has changed in the few years between both pictures. H J Flook's grocery shop is now operated by J H Mills Ltd., and the much cleaner road is now occupied by tramcar 175 on its way into Bristol, a dog-cart with a well dressed man and woman, whilst on the left a country lady is unloading her wares from a horse drawn cart. c1911

Although the quality of this picture is not that good it is necessary for it to be included if for no other reason than it shows on the extreme left without a sunblind, number 67 Regent Street, in the very early days when it first became the "home" of E J Bamford, Ironmonger. For the next seventy years or so it was a cornerstone of Kingswood shopping and became a Mecca for every householder selling products from soaps to paraffin; screws to galvanised baths; gas mantles to electric bulbs, etc. This rank, pictured around 1907, was eventually pulled down to make way for the *Chase Inn*.

Before Moravian Road was widened W. Davis shop stood on the corner, whilst almost opposite was Factory Lane. The small child on a tricycle was too fast for the speed of the camera, as tramcar 188 is about to start the descent all the way to the Tramway Centre. c1903

Mr Davis' shop and adjoining premises have long since disappeared allowing the widening of Moravian Road to take place, as Kingswood bustles about its business on a bright summer afternoon, and it prepares itself for the threatened war against Germany for the second time in living memory. Crossing the road is not yet the hazard it will become with just one parked lorry, a cyclist and two cars in view. c1939

The camera has now been moved even further back in the general direction of Bristol to expose a rank of three shops on the right, the first of which has the name Smith across the front. Moravian Road has yet to be widened, the entrance to Halls Road can just be seen on the right. Regent Street itself looks remarkably deserted and dirty. c1904

Once again the camera has been moved in the same direction, this time to reveal the Swaish emporium. Flowers are sold on the corner of Halls Road; a small white dog sniffs around the mud scattered along the somewhat deserted Regent Street, whilst three young boys stand at the edge of the pavement watching with interest the strange man with his tripod. c1904

W G Plucknett was a prolific photographer in the Kingswood area, and appeared to be delighted in taking pictures of the Whitsuntide processions, probably in the hope of conjuring up more trade. Very often those that survive are difficult to date with any form of accuracy, but the picture on the right is clearly identified on the back of the card as "Whitsuntide treat, Kingswood, 28th May 1928". Taken in Regent Street near to the junction with Downend Road.

In the warm May sunshine another procession marches along Regent Street, and passes Downend Road, helped on this occasion with a band playing stirring music much to the enjoyment of the onlookers. Although not certain, it is believed that the date of the photograph is around 1912, and that the band could be the YMCA's. Note the sign on the right, which reads, "Electric Cars Stop here if requested"

It would appear that once again, Mr Plucknett has leaned out of his studio window and taken another parade picture, possibly the end of the procession as young children are crammed into horse-drawn carts like sardines. In the background, the driver of tram 179 keeps his charge under control, whilst no doubt being very concerned over maintaining his timetable, on the way to the Tramway Centre. c1907

Looking up Regent Street from the corner of Downend Road, during the mid 1950's. The surgery of the late Dr. Grace is on the left, next to the Odeon Cinema, all sadly lost when the Chase Shopping Centre was constructed. Note the F W Woolworth shop on the right.

Regent Street is seen in one of its quiet moods from a position close to the junction with Downend Road. Just one or two pedestrians stroll along in the warm sunshine; two young lads lean over a bicycle, whilst a heavy ladened handcart approaches the camera. c1906

With the photographer having moved his equipment back a few yards, and re-positioned the angle, the junction with Downend Road can now be clearly seen, as can the properties on the right. c1907

REGENT ST KINGSWOOD

This is a more modern view of the area surrounding the junction of Regent Street with Downend Road, busy with pedestrians, but not so busy with motor vehicles, in fact there is not one car to be seen, and crossing the road would have been so much easier. c1952

REGENT STREET, KINGSWOOD

Probably less than ten years separate these two views of Regent Street, but already there is an increase in the number of private cars on show, and the street furniture is beginning to dominate the scene. c1960

The Kingswood Wesleyan Sunday School banner is held aloft as, with a local band, they proudly march along Regent Street, having just passed Brunt's Store, on the corner of Downend Road c1958,

Having moved further along Regent Street, we have with this picture gone back in time by more than half a century. Young lads, in front of C H Cordys Provision Store, strike up a pose that is so reminiscent of the period; with private houses to the right, and the YMCA to the left. The few people visible in this picture all appear to be dressed in black, which might indicate that Queen Victoria has recently died, or it could just be that they are wearing winter black. c1903.

Two Mile Hill, Kingswood. near Bristol.

An Aerial view of Cross Street as seen from its junction with Soundwell Road, curving upwards to its junction with Downend Road. A corner of Grantham Road can be seen on the right, as can Victoria Park as it stretches diagonally towards the top right-hand corner of the picture. c1966.

A couple, with what might be a Barrel Organ, take their load across the top of Downend Road, whilst behind them, a carter holds the head of the lead horse, pulling a load of fresh cut timber. Tram 180 heads on into Bristol having regained the single track; note the fine tracery work employed by the Victorians in the construction of the posts used to hold the electric wires. c1904.

Regent St Kingswood

Yet another of Mr Plucknett's picture of a Whitsuntide procession, taken from the window of his studio, although on this occasion he has directed the camera towards Bristol. The majority of the marchers are women, with a few children, as no men appear in this group, which might indicate that they are all members of a particular women's institution. In these circumstances they are ideally passing Mrs A Wiltshire's boot and shoe shop. Beyond is A P Roberts pastry shop; Henry Playfair, and S Powell. Note the sign on the tram post warning of the procession. c1925

A similar view but one which was taken many years previously, and one which quite clearly shows the change in fashion, particularly with regard to the ladies, and also the much greater level of support and involvement. Not only are there many people lining the route, nearly every window contains more onlookers. This picture really does encapsulate part of our social history that will never be seen again. c1908

On the left is another evocative picture as, with banner aloft, the Kingswood ladies parade themselves dressed all in white and wearing their best sunbonnets. On the back of the card it has been written *"next to shop, W Cook; E Gay; A Davis, and H Mortimer"*, but it does not say which shop, do these names mean anything to anyone? Beneath the banner Peacock's shop is holding a clearance sale, is this the shop mentioned above? c1908.

It is now the turn of the men to march along in the late spring sunshine, looking so much more sober and weary in their dark suits, despite the presence of the band, than the ladies do in the above picture. With, what appears to be the local vicar in front pushing his bike, they all look as they pass 27 and 29 Regent Street as though they are on their way to a funeral, rather than the celebration of the Whitsuntide. c1907

Almost certainly this is not one of Mr Plucknett's pictures but is included to give a distinct and separate view of the procession, as it marches passed the stationery pony and trap, with the Two Mile Hill Evangel Sunday School banner being proudly carried at its head. On the right is a glimpse of J H Green's hosier shop next to Peacock's china; glass, and drapery shop. c1904.

A working day view of Regent Street, with A J Jackson, Boot and Shoe Machinery Engineering Works at 26 Regent Street on the left, whilst tramcar 185 is on its way to the Tramway Centre, and a group of men standing outside Parkers Dairy watching the day go by. c1905

In the middle right of this photograph is the façade of the aptly named "REGENT STREET PICTURE HOUSE" situated next to the even more impressive façade of the Kingswood Engineering Works, adorned with heavy carving and two small signs, one of which advertises Vacuum Oils, and the other states G. W. K. Cycle Clips. Only horse vehicles appear in this c1905 view.

The same façade has by now been modified to accommodate the new fangled requirements of the internal combustion engine, with a variety of petrol from different companies to choose from. Not only that, you can buy the latest Ford model, and have it serviced and/or repaired inside the building. c1954.

This Aerial view shows the heart of Kingswood, with Downend Road cutting a swath from left to right before its junction with Regent Street. New shops have begun to appear at this point, but the mass of the Odeon Cinema still dominates its surroundings. The many terraced houses in Victoria Park; Unity Street; South Road; Moravian Road; Laurel Street, and Bright Street are clearly shown, as Kingswood meets Bristol. c1966

Three very similar but also very different views of Regent Street as it approaches the junction with South Road. Top left:. on a sunny afternoon with just one motor car (MF9715), and many pedestrians enjoying the benefits of shopping in Kingswood.(c1927) Above HW2093 has parked right on the corner, but whose to stop him? certainly not the little baby in the pram. (c1925) Bottom left: A much more up-to-date picture basically showing the same view, with less pedestrians and an increase in traffic both private and public. 28th August 1986.

The same junction in the opposite direction, with the Midland Railway Offices on the right above the local newspaper shop and the adjoining Gents hairdresser, gas street lighting, a few people strolling around, and a solitary tram heading into Bristol. c1906. Below left, the No 87 bus begins to leave Kingswood behind as it heads for Filton during October 1981, whilst on the same day, the camera has been turned completely around, and shows a constant stream of traffic in both directions, none of which are legally allowed to park along the street now that the yellow lines have been painted, and parking restrictions enforced. Note the narrow entrance to Victoria Park on the right, just to the left of the small group of conversationalists standing outside of Julian Flook's wine shop.

As the First World War soldiers became more and more bogged down in the trenches of Flanders during the second year of that conflict, in March 1916 Kingswood and the surrounding areas experienced on the night of the 27/28th its heaviest snowstorm for some while, as shown in these two views of the damage caused along Regent Street. The snow, accompanied with gale force winds started at around 6.00pm on the Monday evening and lasted well into the following Tuesday morning and, as can be seen above, brought down telephone poles and wires, with some falling across the electric tram wires and causing them to short out, resulting in trams being stranded, (see left-hand picture) and unable to get beyond Whiteways Road, from the city.

Two Mile Hill Road and Zion Chapel, Kingswood.

This trio of pictures shows above a greetings card prepared by R J Hill, photographer of Regent Street, of the premises of Kyght ~ saws sharpened and set here. (c1910) On the back of the card it says "My Mom at 10 King Street". Top right shows where Regent Street widens out, with the magnificent frontage of the Zion Free Methodist Chapel, which was opened in 1854, and cost around £2,150 to build. (c1910). Above is a picture of Kingsway Avenue taken on the 28th August 1986.

Cossham Memorial Hospital, Kingswood, Bristol. 1432.

Above is a peep at the opening ceremony of Cossham Hospital on the 1st June 1907, with a picture of the full frontage of the building, (c1911) whilst below is Kingswood "Castle" situated off Lodge Hill and near Hopewell Hill, and originally a windmill (c1904), whilst on the right is the Kingswood Reformatory and Headmaster's House, (c1912).

Kingswood Reformatory and Head-Maste's House.

Above is the *Warwick Arms* situated on the corner of Charlton Road and King John's Road. Note the Royal Mail letterbox to the right of the ladies, with the VR monogram, which is still in existence. c1904. Above right is tramcar No.7 in wartime livery with the trucks and bumpers painted white, whilst the destination box has been painted black, stopping on the way to Kingswood, along the Two Mile Hill at the junction with Charlton Road. c1940. Below is the frontage of the Kingsway Cinema, with two young children about to enter, possibly to see the Saturday morning show. On the left, a mother and daughter check the coming events. c1950

This aerial view shows a close up of Seymour Road, Cross Street and the back of Kennington Avenue area, with a glimpse of the houses fronting part of Soundwell Road. Large factory buildings dominate the rows of terraced properties, but a small copse of trees help to bring in an important green space. c1966